The Sagittarius who was afraid to love

José Micard Teixeira

This book was written with you in mind!

Original title – O Sagitário que tinha medo de Amar

1st Edition - April 2024

Author - José Micard Teixeira

Translator – Ingrid Koehler Micard Teixeira

ISBN – 9798329428780

One of the phrases that struck me most from my grandfather was when he told me to be like the sun and learn to shine on my own. I remember he said it with an open smile and emphasized that relying on me before relying on others gave me the advantage of being able to choose first whatever I decided to choose, whatever made the most sense to me, whatever was my freedom and my freedom alone. You don't want to belong to anything, he continued, because belonging is the same as losing yourself. Be free and only accept into your life those who respect and make your freedom grow. Anyone who wants to take it away from you doesn't deserve you, because they don't understand that only someone who is free can truly love. It's impossible to love without being free, just as you can't love without respecting yourself at the same time. My grandfather used to speak to me like a sage. Like a messenger from something greater than himself. Like someone who knew what was in store for me.

Sometimes I need to be alone, far away from everyone, left to my own devices, listening to myself without needing to speak, thinking about what I'm feeling and feeling what I'm thinking. It doesn't happen often, but when it does, something in me asks for change, new paths, new faces, different places, unknown smells, unexplored shores and unseen storms. In fact, when I want to be alone, it's because something in me is already changing, still imperceptible, but foreseen through thoughts that escape me like winds without direction. I'm not scared. On the contrary. I let them gradually take over who I still am so that they can transform me into who I want to be, as if in a perfect symbiosis, like a disobedient hurricane that tears up seas and crushes waves and, in the end, leaves a trail of strange calm. In fact, there is a tranquility inherent in this whole process of change, not only because it is calm, but also because I am a traveler dressed in calmness and memories of peace. I stopped being afraid a long time ago. I've learnt to accept change as the cure for all my lack of answers.

I'm going to live a long life. I know this not because it was told to me in words, but only because I felt a voice touch my chest and make it feel like a certainty. I didn't need anything else. There are certain things that you realize are true without needing proof. They have your energy, your essence, your skin, and they touch your soul like a kiss, like the most meaningful word of all, the one you've never heard, but which you recognize as being for you and no one else. Whoever said it to me didn't identify themselves. They told me what they had to tell me and then disappeared, leaving me teary-eyed as if they had revealed some secret only shared by angels. I cried with joy for a long time and only lost my smile when I began to question what I had heard. There are certain things you should never doubt. They come from a place that belongs to you and to which you will one day return. They come from someone who knows you better than you could ever imagine. Things from heaven. Things made of love.

Not being loved as a child is like putting salt on an open wound. It hurts as if it was normal. It burns as if burning was the condition for feeling alive. It burns as if burning was the strangest way to believe in any kind of love. The days are nothing more than nights with little light and the nights are as long as the silences and indifference, like everything that you only later realize was missing, like everything that you only later realize never existed. Not being loved when you're a child is to create memories in you that smell of pain and tears, it's to make you grow up with a strange desire to ignore and run away from what you wish could be reconstructed today with other colors and angles, it's to leave marks that no surgeon can disguise, it's to never be allowed to smile the smile that you'll hardly ever be able to smile again with the freest side of your soul. To be unloved as a child is to be made into an adult afraid to feel, to be forever forbidden to shine, to be imprisoned in what we will always fear, in what will make us crawl all our lives because we ignore having wings. It's killing what few will have the courage to live. It's making us believe that God doesn't have a heaven for us too.

Let's belong to each other forever, halves of a whole that always wants more, parts of a world that is the exact size of our embrace. Let's be encounters that promote our most beautiful smiles and our most tender kisses. Let's be secrets that only we know, eternities that last a single second, let's dance dances in silence and die in life the times our love decides to kill us for loving each other endlessly. Let's be angels, the kind who don't need wings because they're more than angels, the kind who don't need to speak to hear what they want most, the kind who love each other as if loving was simply staying. Let's always be me and you and you and me, as if no one else existed and no one else dared to exist between us, because that's what loving is too, it's blinding ourselves so that we don't see anything we don't want to, it's blinding ourselves so that we only see ourselves whenever we want to.

There are days when I let myself be taken back to the time when I would have liked to have been happy and I wasn't, not to suffer or complain, but to imagine what it would have been like if everything had been different. It's hard for a five-year-old to realize that there's more to life than what they're experiencing at that moment. It's only later that they realize what was missing and what should never have existed or happened. For me, my father and mother were my world, that cocoon where I sought security and where, I realize today, there was only the cocoon, that place that made me feel like a spare part, alone, always clutching a teddy bear as if I wanted to receive from it what I didn't know but felt I was missing. Today, I imagine what it would be like if I didn't need that rag doll so much and felt more my parents' arms around me, their hugs, kisses and smiles, if they spoke to me in that sweet, melodious voice they use to speak to babies, even if I didn't understand much of what they were saying to me, because a child doesn't need to know words, but to feel the way they are said, how they reach their heart and make them feel protected, loved and important. Today, I wonder what it would be like if I had felt their love while growing up, how I wouldn't be so afraid of it without letting those around me know, how I wouldn't run away from it so much because I knew perfectly well what it meant. Today, perhaps I wouldn't have suffered so much if I'd realized earlier that the problem wasn't with me, but with them, with those who raised me and didn't know how to love or love themselves. Today would certainly be different, but I don't know if I would love myself more than I do today.

My path hasn't been easy at all, but I wouldn't change a moment or a choice, a word not said or repeated too much, a pointless complaint or a few furtive tears shed in the darkness of my room, the many mistakes that often resulted in consequences that were difficult to resolve and accept, the loves I thought I felt and were disappointed by, the places I chose and almost let myself die in. I went through long and painful phases, simply because I didn't believe in myself enough, or in my power to choose differently and take more risks. I suffered, but it was worth it, because it was a suffering made up of blessings and lessons, of losses and pains that forced me to finally think about myself one day, to realize that I had everything to be who I truly was and that the person preventing me from being that was just me and nobody else, as I had believed for far too long. My path hasn't been easy, but I wouldn't know how to live another one, not just because this is the one I've known, but because it's certainly the one I've chosen and wouldn't hesitate to choose again, because I've learnt with age that there are things that shouldn't be changed despite all the pain they cause, things that can no longer be changed, things that are no longer worth rewriting on the walls of other people's houses because they would bring consequences that I don't know about and that I certainly wouldn't want to experience. My path wasn't easy, but the result was worth it. It has given me a smile of life and a pair of wings to fly without fear over what used to throw me to the ground.

It's wonderful when we realise that we're changing for the better, when something in us gives rise to a joy almost of recognition, of gratitude, when for a moment life seems to be in tune with us or we with it, it doesn't matter, because it's a state of unparalleled awareness and happiness. We were born to evolve through loving ourselves, respecting our choices, the way we allow others to treat us, and then giving others who we are in order to fulfil our purpose in this life. Unfortunately, we more easily choose to evolve through suffering, not because we want to, but because we don't love ourselves enough to manage otherwise. We believe much more in others than in ourselves and rarely question the reason for suffering. We'd rather suffer than love. It may sound stupid, but it's true. We are too attached to dogmas and lies to be able to see what many people do everything they can to prevent us from seeing. We need to have the courage to feel and follow what we feel. We need to start listening more to our soul and following what it asks of us, not because we want to believe it's best for us, but because we know it's what will take us to our heaven on earth. It's as simple as that. Like a smile after tears.

I've got used to taking up the whole bed when I go to sleep, to spreading my legs without feeling anyone next to me, to waking up on my own without someone asking me for something I don't feel like giving them in the middle of the night, to getting up and showering on my own for as long as I want, to preparing my breakfast with a damp towel wrapped around my waist, to singing out loud without being told to shut up because their head hurts, without being told that I'm just selfish, without them turning away spitting words of contempt. I've got used to not having to explain myself to any living being and choosing to do what I like without having to ask any soul for permission, to cancelling appointments at short notice simply because I've become the master of my own time and will, to lingering wherever I want and leaving as soon as I feel like it from places that bore me or don't mean anything to me. I've got used to my things, to myself and my life, to my silence and the sound of my music, to the pit in my sofa and the cookie crumbs on my shirt, to being in my own company without being afraid of being alone or needing anyone else's company, to feeling and realizing that this isn't loneliness, but simply the joy of being able to be happy with myself without needing anyone else's presence. There are things you learn late, but still just in time to live them without regrets. Without forced forgetfulness. With almost nothing, because in fact they have become almost everything.

I wake up in the morning and sometimes it still seems strange that I don't have to go to an office where I spent hours of real torture doing what had nothing to do with me, where I dedicated a substantial part of my life working on exhausting tasks that never ceased to seem detestable, living with people who mostly didn't act like people, but like abominable creatures whose only interest was to please those who despised them. Now, I wake up in the morning and smile because I had the courage to say 'no' to the suffering imposed on me by others, to a meaningless life where goals were always condemned, to a whirlwind of numbers, decisions, profits, frustrations and fears and, above all, to a time lost in the search for a new time where the air that asphyxiated me was not mine, but imposed on me by those who never had anything to do with me. Now, I wake up in the morning and know that what awaits me was created by me and by the hand of my god, that everything is the result of my choices in the face of my greatest fears, that I was born to help others not to stay where I probably stayed for too long. Now, I wake up in the morning and I know that it's life that wakes me up and not the clock, that it's me who gets out of bed and not a man dominated by fear and frustration, that I deserve everything that happens to me because one day I decided to believe that waking up free should be one of the most majestic sensations one could aspire to. It's as simple as that.

Today I woke up without me. I felt like I had no reason to get up, no strength to get out of bed, no will to face everything once again, no sense of what I've been losing every day that I force myself to be who I don't want to be, without that glimmer of joy that makes me want to watch the sunrise from my bedroom window every time I open the blinds, without being able to say anything, clinging to my pillow as if that was all I had left in life, and I found myself crying a silent cry that quickly turned into a sob of despair, a gagged scream in the depths of my throat, an asphyxiation that I seemed to get used to without feeling short of breath, an arrhythmia that threw my heart from one side of my chest to the other in a frightening silence, unheard with every beat, mysteriously agitated in all its wreckage without memories. Without needing to think too much, I realized that something in me wasn't right, not physically, but inside my mind, inside that intricate maze of tired neurons reluctant to let me up, reminding me of fears and words impossible to write, begging me to give up wanting to insist, whispering to me to let myself stay, to call someone so they could take me where they could look after me, where they could give me what they no longer knew how to give me, where I could finally close my eyes without my eyelids hurting, where I could once again give colours to what I still want to believe in, where I wouldn't feel put off by so much procrastination. I cried non-stop for an eternity. I grabbed my mobile phone and called you. At that moment, I just wanted to hear your voice, because I know that only you have the ability to quiet everything in me that seems to want to die, to leave, to go mad, to break forever. Only you and nobody else. At times, not even my angels. Not even those who would take care of bringing me back from now on.

I'm well into my sixties, but I don't feel old at all. I feel that I'm as old as I want to be, that age when I can decide to go on a trip from one moment to the next and choose the country I'm going to visit just by circling the globe, I feel that I'm at that age when I can have a birthday every day just because I feel like celebrating life, that age when I feel everything more calmly and deeply, with more intimacy and desire, with more certainties than hopes. When I was young, I believed that someone in their sixties had neither the energy nor the will for anything other than waiting for their death. Today, I smile and I know that each person's age is revealed by the light that emanates from them, by the easy smile they let draw on their face when they meet someone in the middle of the street, by the courage to go where few still dare to go, by the beauty of not choosing friends by the amount of wrinkles or grey hair, by the audacity to believe that they can kiss with the same passion as when they were twenty. Being over sixty is a blessing that some reach without any great stories to tell, but it's also a time when many still fall madly in love, when they experience incredible love without any rules, when they dance alone in the rain without fear of catching a cold, when they can talk about whatever they want even if no one listens. To be over sixty and not be afraid of growing old is to recognize that what is wonderful doesn't necessarily have to be unforgettable and what is unforgettable doesn't necessarily have to be remembered. It's measuring everything not by its duration or memory, but by the intensity with which some small things can still make your breath and your heart beat accelerate without necessarily making you sad or killing you.

I know who you are, not so much because of what you tell me you are, but because of how you make me feel every time you look at me with those green eyes and kiss me without saying a word. Your mouth is not just another woman's mouth, but rather two banks of water and thirsty flesh, two scars created by the kisses you gave without love before you met me, that you gave without desire or passion, that you gave because you were asked to look like a woman. I come from a place where the trains have fallen asleep and the moon never drops below the horizon. It stays up there like a star, casting a fleeting shadow over your eyelashes while we kiss attached to nothing but ourselves, like two people who love each other even more with every touch of the tongue between the teeth and gums, in the wild way the hair is devoured, in the fingers that grip the chin firmly so that none of the words that are spoken between moans and sighs of life are understood. When I pull away, I know that one mouth only waits for another, but ours wait for something that no one else can have, they wait for a dance between eyes and shoulders, between arms and chest, in mute consent for another shock of fury when we come together again, suffocating, without form or existence, entwined by the certainty that there is no greater love than that which is made up of madness and a lot of madness. The kiss ends as if it wasn't going to end, because our bodies continue to kiss without lips or tongues, but with fingers and hands, with skin and words that are difficult to say, words that only the sound of non-existent violins can make audible to our ears for a brief moment. I love you as I've never loved anyone else and I know that you love me as only mermaids know how. With salt. With the sea. With necklaces of seashells and whelks resting between shy smiles on my thighs.

You would be ninety today if you were still alive, if that terrible illness hadn't shortened your life and the time you still deserved to live among us and especially with me. I'm not being selfish. I'm just calling for a time that would surely have been different after your illness made us be closer to each other. I had to wait more than fifty years to hear you say that you liked being with me, to feel your hand resting on my thigh to confess that you felt safe with me by your side in the IPO[1], to ask me if I would come and visit you the next day when you were sent home to die with your family. During that time, I could see a gleam in your eyes that was dulled by pain and fever, but still intense, almost of admiration for the son you hadn't understood or wanted or been able to understand all your life. I often wonder what it would have been like from then on if you hadn't left, if we could have started a new life again from that moment on, if you would have accepted me with earrings and tattoos, if you would have laughed with me at my crazy behaviour, which, deep down, you could well have

---

[1] IPO = Portuguese Institute of Oncology.

done yourself, because what united me to you was that similar energy we shared, that essence of adventure and freedom, of travelling to the other side of the world without suitcases and without fear, that essence that made me love you with such intensity even though I felt it was probably only one-sided. In fact, I don't know if you ever loved me, but in those weeks before your death you showed me something different, a conscious sense of who I was, an understanding that I was more than just a son, that I was also a collection of cells that came from your body, tiny but enough to give you a feeling of recognition, of connection, a desire to go further and to finally accept my kiss and my embrace, just a few days before you said goodbye without speaking a single word to me, leaving with your eyes fixed on the ceiling, not as if you were looking at infinity, but rather as if you were seeing your father and mother with open arms to take you in and give you the love they never knew how to give you. That's why I loved you. That's why I forgave you. That's why I feel you close to me every day.

My greatest sadness is that I can't socialize with my youngest daughter when I want to. She's the fruit of a relationship that didn't work out, but I feel an enormous love for her that I can hardly put into words. Every day I pray for us and remember little episodes that we experienced in the few times we were together, even under sick and dysfunctional control. We have a connection that's more akin to angels dancing at their source, a father-daughter connection that's unfiltered, natural, akin to the princes and princesses in your children's books that you sometimes ask me to buy for you. I was forced to make decisions that my soul was asking me to make, but that my heart didn't want to accept. Sometimes you have to say No so that one day the moon will shine again freely, intensely, even without having to create any moonlight.

My grandfather once told me that the worst thing that can happen to a man is to fall in love with two women at the same time. I remember looking at him without understanding why he was saying such a thing to me. Later, I realized that he was talking about himself. When he died, there was talk of there being another woman in his life, a woman my grandmother knew existed and who also did nothing to stop it. It's true that those were different times, but I was able to understand the role of each of them in this love triangle. My grandmother couldn't give my grandfather everything he needed and she had a very different way of being in life from him. They got on well, but shared a secret that generally brought neither pain nor suffering, just an understanding that surpassed much that few can comprehend. The only one who eventually suffered was my grandfather because he had to divide himself between his conscience, his heart and his desires. I'm not criticizing him or my grandmother. Love isn't always just a feeling. Often, it's also loving to the point of consenting to what isn't supposed to exist.

When you start to experience true love, you start to deal with all your greatest fears at the same time. It can't be otherwise when you start to love. We were almost all brought up to trust no one but God. We were all taught not to trust strangers. If we've never been truly loved, everyone we love is a real stranger at first. It's someone who comes to test everything that is most fragile and insecure in us, someone who comes to show us the extent of our struggle with ourselves. It's someone who has come to control our emotions and make us feel lost. If we don't have self-respect, we won't be able to withstand the challenges of love, the suffering, the uncertainty, the impression of being in someone else's hands. You have to trust, you have to surrender, you have to stop being afraid of suffering. Love is the only way to live. Outside of it, everything is an illusion created by lies we tell ourselves to avoid suffering for love. It's as simple as that.

Leave everything and come with me. Don't be afraid. I'm not going to hurt you. I'm just going to show you what you've never been allowed to see. Come with me without thinking too much. Follow your will and let me show you how everything is different from what you believe. There's a world beyond your world, a world where anything is possible, where there are more stars than words, where silence shines brighter than the sun, where every step you take is the measure of your daring. Come with me and don't ask anything. Just come as if I was your guide in the middle of an inhospitable but beautiful forest. Come and smile. My world will become yours too. Forever.

Today, I just want to lie on the sand, without a towel, close to where the waves break and feel the sun warm my skin. Today, I don't feel like doing anything other than enjoying a day in peace. The mobile phone stayed at home. The world stayed on my computer and I fled here. I don't care about anything else.

Forgive me, but today I'm going to devote myself to myself. Call me what you like, say what you like about my attitude, but today I'm going to give myself a day without thinking about anything that takes my peace away.

It's funny how lately I hear so much about impossible loves. People seem to want to fantasize about unattainable things as a way of escaping the failure of their relationships. Everything they know they'll never have becomes eternal in its absence. Love is supposed to have a strong connection with the inextinguishable. It needs to sound like something forever, otherwise it doesn't make any sense. Until death do you part. An impossible love is a forever love. It can stay in your heart until it happens. And because it doesn't happen, the delirium lasts as long as the unrealizable persists. This is what impossible love is. A legal way to dream without suffering.

In loving, love is the commitment. Love is the secret of the duration of love. When two people love each other, they're not doing it for either of them, but for both of them. Sometimes it's forgotten that to love is to build love. It's not about sharing something that already exists, but about building something new. Those who love know that verbalizing love gives memory to feelings. It allows us to know the connection between each person and each other. Those who love don't die. They choose to take responsibility for their love until they die.

At the age of sixty-two, I've realised that I've become a man of short, intense things. I no longer have the patience for long, boring and repetitive things. I want to experience everything quickly, passionately and freely. I've long since stopped devoting time to those who complicate, lie and disrespect. Some people accuse me of being selfish, but the truth is that I believe that selfishness is the first form of self-love, in my own philosophy that I can only give who I am. If I don't know how to love myself, I won't know how to love others, but only how to need them. If I don't respect myself, I won't know how to respect anyone and I'll permanently allow disrespect into my life. I have these things. I only want what's best for me.

I remember perfectly the last look my father gave me before he died. It was a look lost in a darkness that only he could see, a look that showed an endeavour to glimpse me through the shadows that must have been clouding his view. He didn't hear the last words I said to him before he left, of that I'm sure, because there was a strange, painful emptiness in his eyes as he looked in the direction of the person who was speaking to him. His forehead was cold and he didn't even react the way he used to when I kissed him. His eyes searched mine one last time before I left him sitting on the sofa in the living room. I don't know if he saw me at that moment. What I do know is that he stared at me for a few seconds, serious, as if he finally recognized me, and then he let them rise slowly, as if he was serenely indicating where he was ready to go.

Feeling that someone regrets many of the choices they've made in their life gives me a sadness equal to that of a loss. Don't regret anything you've done. If you don't like the result, take a different direction today. No one can defeat your spirit but you. Don't give others power over your life. Choose. Decide. Take hold. Let go. Cry. Shout. Fall down. Get up. Move forward, but never give up on yourself. Never forget that you are the most important person in your life.

I want to grow old with joy. I want to live each day I have left with the serenity of someone who understands a little more about life than they ever thought they would. Death no longer scares me. I believe I'm going where I'm supposed to go, where I've never really stopped being. I live each thing I have to live in its own moment, even those that make me suffer or cry, because I know that everything I attract is part of who I am and who I want to be. I'm grateful for what I learn, and I realized a long time ago that the important thing is not so much what I learn, but whether I live according to what I've learnt. Age has made me realize that I shouldn't demand anything of myself and only want to do my part before I leave. I became free by my choices and I want to live and celebrate my freedom until my last day. I don't know how to live any other way. I don't want to live any other way.

Surviving can't be a mission, or even a purpose. When you survive, you inevitably abandon your mission and purpose. You know that without a mission and purpose, nothing happens or is created. The truth is that everything that repeats itself without you wanting it to almost always exists with suffering. So stop to feel who you are and where you are heading. Realize once and for all that your true story is written only on the skin of your soul.

Believe that I'm not the one who will understand you, get to know you or be with you when you need it most. Believe that I'm not the one who's going to support you, forgive you or watch over you in your sleep. Believe that I'm not the one who's going to love you the way you want to be loved, know your time and your lack of time, tell you that everything is fine or take you on my journeys. If you thought you knew me, maybe I fooled you without really wanting to. Forgive my choice, but I'm too attached to my freedom to jeopardize it for anyone. Maybe you'll never understand me. Maybe you'll never believe me. I beg you to not wish me harm. Don't hate me or change the idea you've created of me. It's not your fault. The truth is that I didn't deceive you. The truth is that I discovered through you that I want something that only I can give me.

What's not good for me, I don't need.

I always find it easy to smile. I have no trouble smiling at all. I believe that many people who don't smile blame others for not being able to. This is normal, because not everyone has the capacity to accept the powerlessness of not doing something. I think they forget too easily that a smile can change a life.

I'm addicted to curable pain. I have addictions to loving grammar and emotional algebra. I have addictions that make me cry with rage because I realize how powerless I am to ignore them. I have addictions that live between my skin and your words and grow in an alchemy without brakes or rules. They don't kill me. They don't weaken me. They don't overwhelm me. They invade me like a fever. They gag me like a silence. They numb me like a drug. I have addictions that I don't share with anyone, simply because I believe that every addiction has a secret that longs to become a love story without reasons or excuses. I have addictions and I know how to live in the middle of them, just as I've learnt to live in the middle of the space between your absence and my body.

If someone hurts you, don't choose to be like the person who hurt you. If someone hurts you, don't do the same things as them. Always remember that life tests you to your limits so that you understand who you can or can't be. What life asks of you is coherence. What life asks of you is that you never stop being yourself and always avoid being what others provoke you to be. Concentrate only on your transformation. The rest is only what others choose to think and be towards you.

Love begins in the innocence of an encounter. I saw you without knowing you were seeing me. I seduced you without knowing you were seducing me. Before you, I didn't realize there could be so much charm in a smile. Before you, I didn't know that feelings didn't need reasons or motives to happen. I called you mine before you were even mine. I loved you before I even knew it. I possessed you before I even touched you. You brought poetry with you and the sea in your eyes. You became the beach and the tide of my heart. You made me believe once again in the light beyond the light and you became the destiny of my love. I became yours so that you could be mine and let me love you as I pleased, without haste. You let yourself be taken by me. You let yourself fall asleep in my arms. I promise not to close my eyes.

It's only others who come to give us lessons. We don't learn anything on our own. It's in relationships with others that we recognize and transform ourselves. It's through them that we can feel our original energy, the energy that brought us here with a mission and a purpose that are very clear, but still quite imprecise for many of us. It's in relationships that we finally realize that our path can become less lonely than it has been until now.

It's okay if you fail. Failure is also learning. Don't worry if it hurts. Nobody likes to fail. Work through the pain and don't mind if you become sad. Sadness happens when you accept why you made that choice rather than any other. Always remember that it's okay to fail, because it means you took a risk. You know that life has no meaning if you don't risk following what your soul asks of you. You know that only those who take risks can lose their fear of failure. So go ahead. Take a risk. Live your life like you've never lived it before. Feel who you are and don't make any more concessions. The party and the adventure await you.

Always remember that love is nothing more than a conscious surrender between two souls who want to give each other their time and their light. Dare to do everything you want so much and think you'll never achieve. Dare to expand in proportion to your desire not to want to remain the same. Gain strength through your smile, because smiling makes it easier to look fear in the eye. Take one step at a time so that you don't trip over your courage. Never doubt the existence of miracles, because you too are one of them. Believe in yourself and then prepare yourself for the possibility of winning through loss too. Surrender to a power greater than your own every time you feel it in the centre of your heart. Don't be afraid. Don't cower. Trust what you feel. Let yourself go. Believe that you'll never be the same again.

I won the right to do what I want. I eliminated labels and limiting beliefs and began to smile more at myself. I allowed myself to go where I always wanted to go and only come back when I felt like it. I once again felt a joy and freedom that I hadn't felt since I was a kid. I loved every one of my wrinkles and grey hairs from the start. With age, I've become more fun and sensitive to those who love to have fun and feel. I began to rest as if resting was an act of spiritual renewal. I stopped fearing failures and disappointments, because I realized that I'm the one who sees them as such. Whether you like it or not, whether you believe it or not, whether you accept it or not, I'm happy with my life and I intend to stay that way.

I wish you loved me. I know you don't know how much I love you, but I don't mind if you don't either. I dream about you every day, even on the days when I can't fall asleep. It's also true that I don't do much to make myself known to you, perhaps because deep down I fear that even if I did, it wouldn't please you. I'd like you to love me, but I don't think I know how to love the way you'd like to be loved. The truth is that I've never been one of those people who make a lot of sense. I don't always know if I'm in the right place. I haven't won all the fights I've fought, but I know I've lost all the ones I've given up fighting. The truth is, I wish you loved me. I wish I was necessary to you. I wish every moment was forever so I could always love you, but I'm afraid you'll offend me if I tell you about my love one day. I don't want you to humiliate me. You can even ignore me, but I couldn't bear it if you laughed at me. I'd like you to love me, I'd just like you to love me, because if you loved me, maybe I'd also have the courage to tell you how much I love you.

I reject everything that's supposed to be. I reject everything that is imposed on me. I can't stand conditions or hierarchies. All immodesty and false humility irritate me. I find it difficult to accept injustice and prejudice. I find it difficult to materialize friendships and partnerships because they demand of me what I don't want or know how to give them. I'm a loner with an optimistic attitude who tries every day to postpone his mental illness. I'm not crazy, but I love the madness of being thought of as crazy. I'm proud of who I am. I won't change for anyone. I don't care what anyone thinks of me. I do what I want and say what I want. I'm an unashamed rebel. There's nothing I can do about it. I'm going to die smiling.

It's been nine years since you left. Damn, how time flies. Sometimes I still think I have something new to tell you, but then I realize that I can only tell it to you alone. But, you know, I'm very grateful to you for everything you taught me, even if I didn't understand and criticized you at the time. You weren't perfect. You were even a little stubborn, but at some point we're all a little more than we'd like to be. Time has helped me to understand a lot of what you said. Life has shown me that I've learnt what I needed to learn from you. You used to look tough, but more than once I've noticed a tear in the corner of your eye. In that field, I'm just like you, blood of the same blood, heart of the same heart. That's why I'm at peace with myself, even though longing sometimes knocks at the door. That's part of it, you know? But it's also part of smiling for having had you as my father and knowing that one day we'll laugh together again, as if time no longer counted and eternity was our calendar. I hug you once again with a peaceful heart, my Father. May you be smiling too.

I find it difficult to follow others. I'm too independent to stop thinking for myself. I may agree with someone on some points, but I always try to understand what I've heard in the light of who I am. It's not easy to please me, especially as not many people know exactly how to do it. Maybe they imagine me as I'm not. The truth is that I love simplicity and honesty and I'm a fan of people who don't impose anything on me or demand anything. I prefer to choose myself rather than be led or forced to choose, because I believe in my ability to know what's best for me. Even so, I can choose something I don't want, just to please someone I do want. However, I never do it for that person. I always do it for me, for the joy I feel in giving pleasure to those I have chosen to please.

I don't like condescension because it reminds me of a kind of failed pity. I like people who have the attitude and assertiveness to explain without agreeing. There are people who feign weakness in order to get attention and condescension is a safe conduct for their endeavours. I like those who realize this and respect without giving in. I believe it's possible to create a new life from an old one. I argue that everyone is capable of doing this as long as they stop being afraid of the outcome and realise that everything is part of their own path. The problem exists because few people understand the mechanics of life and insist on expecting too much from others. The only certainty we have is that we must walk the path even if we have no certainties at all.

What we need most in people is an open mind to celebrate life more. I know people for whom a joint or a line of cocaine is the gateway to disinhibition and the top of the world. There are people who always make love on the same day and at more or less the same time as if they were taking a medicine or performing a spell. I know men and women who can't live away from their work because it's only there that they feel part of something. I've heard people cry out against the difficulties and refuse a job because of the hours. I know people who are afraid of loneliness and love to gossip and complain about others. But I also know people who like bubble baths, beach parties, Rambo movies, people who aren't afraid to make a fool of themselves with what they like to do, who walk around without underwear, who wear trainers all year round, who don't follow fashions or trends, who don't demand anything from life because they don't care about tomorrow any more than they care about today, who exercise with passion, who listen to music as if they were listening to poetry and who take breaks in life only because they've realized that everything that doesn't stop comes to an end too quickly.

I'm a man of passions and I rarely stay in the same place doing the same thing for long. Sameness bores me. Routine upsets me. Passiveness gets on my nerves. Predictability bores me. I need movement, novelty, challenges, and I love venturing where I haven't ventured before. I need to feel motivated, provoked and stirred up. I always like a bit of madness in my already small amount of caution, so that life always has a flavor of the unexpected. I realized a long time ago that the important thing is to live everything with passion and the full awareness that what matters is just wanting to live. If I don't live everything with the will to do so, I'll let fear take over and I'll be just another person who lives with almost nothing of very little. I refuse to pass by life. Many people don't understand me and criticize me. Maybe that's just the way things are. To hell with it. I believe that life is to be enjoyed and not just tolerated. I reject survival. It scares me.

All changes must come from you. Don't make excuses for putting off a change that you know is important to you. Laziness is resistance to novelty and fear of failure. If you lack determination and courage, remember that it's all part of an even bigger project to make you recognize your strengths and talents. Life tests you because it loves you. Life weakens you so that you can find yourself. Life darkens your day so that you can seek and choose your light. Never doubt this.

I don't believe in people who don't respect me. I have no doubt that nothing they say will ever help or benefit me. When I was a kid, I learned with my father to be suspicious. With age, I've learnt to be cautious instead. This way, I suffer far fewer disappointments and I can more easily get away from these people before their poison enters my veins and makes me say or do something foolish that I will surely regret. Over time, I've realized that in some cases indifference can also be therapeutic.

I like to help those who want to help themselves. I don't lift a finger for those who don't want me to. I don't allow myself to stay with those who want to deceive me so that they can continue to deceive themselves. I no longer allow myself to be easily surprised. I no longer allow myself to be carried away by false sorrows and gaudy joys. I like to look deep into the eyes of the people who come to me and feel what they are really feeling and not want to translate it into words. I'm not always the same in my methods, but I'm always a thoroughbred professional. I don't give up on those who don't want to give up on themselves. I tear my skin off for them. I'll die on watch if necessary. Just because that's who I am. The sum of everything I feel and believe.

A relationship is built on longing. The idea of not being with the person you'd like to be with preserves the feeling. Pain always seems to be present where love is felt. It's an almost stupid duality, but it's undoubtedly one of the conditions for preserving harmony. Opposites attract, but the truth is that they can't destroy themselves. Too much longing leads to want without measure. Too much pain makes you want to forget the feeling. Constant absences tend not to remind us who is no longer missed. There are no great formulas. There's just trial and error. There is learning. And there is the beauty of the quick nostalgia and the long-awaited reunion, which always seems so little but is so much.

I can only remove from my life what I accept as my own. As long as I deny its existence or fight against it, I will never be able to remove it from me. Acceptance means letting what I wish wasn't mine belong to me. If it's with me, it's because it's mine, it's part of what I need to live without fear for it to leave me for good. I only stop fearing what I accept to live. I only stop wanting to feel the same way again once I've understood its meaning in my life. The most important things are always those I can release after suffering at their hands. Everything is lighter without their presence. Everything finally goes your way, no longer out of deceit or suffering. Only in the name of my freedom.

I never miss what I haven't done. Not even what I'm yet to do. I have no urgency about anything. I'm in no hurry to get anywhere. Novelty fascinates me, but I don't look for it. It arises naturally in my life because of my attitude towards the old and used. I can no longer devote my time to what brings me nothing new or stubbornly gives me more of the same. Not everyone understands me, but I don't care whether they do or not. I've reached a point where I no longer feel compassion for those who don't feel it for others. I no longer care about these theories that if I'm not nice, life will take its toll on me. What I decided a long time ago was to respect who I am and who others are, without that implying that I'm a fool enough to allow people to disrespect me. I'm worth more than that. I deserve different. Life thanks me. I know that. I feel it in what it gives me every day. It gives me a unique meaning for everything I accept and reject. Lends me joy and peace.

I can now accept my two ex-wives in peace. Each in their own way revealed in me what I needed to understand about who I wasn't yet. In their own way, they helped me grow in respect for myself. What I thought I lost with them turned out to be a reflection of what I gained. I respect them for what I felt for each of them in their own time, for the children they gave me, for the moments that gave us what we have today. I'm not the same anymore. I couldn't be. The way I see myself today is an extension of what I wasn't able to be and live with them. It could only be like that. I hope they think the same. I really do.

Sometimes I still wonder why I'm only attracted to what's different, to what no one else wants or is looking for. It seems that there is an invisible magnet that leads me to the strangest places and to the people who are the most different from me, even if they are similar in some way. I always approach the most difficult thing, the thing that makes me want to achieve it. I find it hard to accept what's easy. I always believe that it's short-lived and won't keep me interested for long. I like what makes me feel what I've never felt before, what I've probably feared too much and for no reason. I can't stand sameness and a lack of passion, the schedules and precepts. It seems that a voice is secretly telling me to run away from them like the devil runs away from the cross. It's not a question of fear. It's a question of me. Mine alone. It's part of my centaur side. My planet Venus stuck in the house of Scorpio. Bold, like that. Like me, with me.

I'd like to read the palm of your hand and discover my name written on the lifeline. I'd like to lift my eyes and realize that yours are closed while you listen to me read. I wish I could touch your hair and tell you a future that was ours. I find it hard to talk to you about things I don't want to see between the bumps and the lines of your hands. I'm afraid you'll only see me as the one who tells you about presents and possible tomorrows. I wish you weren't indifferent to the way I hold your fingers and run my trembling finger along your palm. I wish the smell of your perfume would give me the courage to tell you things that only my heart knows. Maybe you'd pull your hand out of mine and leave. Maybe you'd never come back. Maybe you'd hate me. But I would have told you about my love. I would have told you about the need to forget what I feel. Not as if it was nothing, but as if everything could still be.

I don't waste a day of my life. I know that each one is being offered to me so that I can make a difference. I make the most of it, because it's in making the most of each day that I show that I accept that everything lasts only as long as it has to and leaves the mark it has to. I enjoy each day, not as if it was the first or the last, but as if it was unrepeatable. I enjoy each day, but without wanting to make it the key to my happiness, because that lies in my attitude. Each moment is magical if I can see and feel its magic. Each moment is a challenge for me to live what comes next. Every minute can be worth an incarnation as long as I am consciously grateful to be living it. I receive what each person has to give me and I don't run away from feeling what I'm feeling when I receive it. I've realized that heaven toasts on my behalf every time I choose to face something rather than endure it.

In a relationship, trust is not the purpose, but simply the assumption. Lack of trust hurts, even when there's no reason for it. It's a wound without a bandage. Time without breath. A defence without a strategy. If there is no trust, there is fear. If I live in fear, I move away from my path. And I don't want that. If it hurts, I want to know why it hurts. I need to look the truth right in the eyes. I need to be at peace. Those who are with me owe me that, or I'll leave. I immediately realize that the search is elsewhere, on another horizon. I stopped being afraid of the unknown a long time ago. I pack my bag and leave. I return home. I lie down on the sofa and let myself fall asleep. There's no one like me. I'm sure of it.

I'm sixty-two years old and I often find myself thinking incredulously about my departed friends. They're still so vivid in my memories that it seems like a lie, a figment of my imagination or a recent nightmare that keeps filling my head. The truth is that I realize that we are all inevitably going to die one day and that idea doesn't leave me indifferent. In those moments, I wonder about many things, about what they felt at the moment of their death, if they suffered, where they are, if eternity is the truth, if I'm part of this whole puzzle or just the fruit of a hallucination so real that it leads me to question all of this for no clear reason. Death doesn't scare me, but I don't know how I'll cope with physical suffering. I've seen brave people groan in pain. I've seen happy people cry to contain their grief. I've seen angels bend over their chests to stifle the scream that tears at their flesh and soul. I don't want to think about it too much either. I've learned that I have to live day to day in my own way, without fear, with a smile on my lips, always compassionate towards those who suffer, but never surrendered to the fear of an end that I can't control, an end that I believe will be done in peace and in my own company instead. I've always thought that it's better to die alone, without the possibility of causing pain to anyone else. To die only with ourselves and with our eyes turned towards eternity. Embracing the light with the stillness of all returns made only to make us smile.

I gave you the moon because I know how much you love moonlight. I really want you to remember me every time the sky takes on the clarity of early January nights, where the mists mix with the last rays of the sun like shadows with your movements around me. I couldn't give you less, because you don't deserve less. You give me more than a thousand moons. You give me the smiliest smile in the world, a smile that makes me discover in myself what only you allow me to see, sides and angles of me that God created for you to reveal to me, not as a prophecy to be fulfilled, but rather as a story with no need for a title or a path. I gave you the moon because it brings out the soft green of your eyes, that colour that only angels can have, that colour that few can see as I see them. They are eyes of love, eyes that see the world before me and then reveal it to me without lack of hope, they read it to me like a poem and a secret together, looking at me in that silence that only words can repeat. The moon slowly searches for the place of your eyes. It lands with simplicity and paints them an even more olive colour, around the iris, like a painting made where you want to stay, a canvas that reflects what you want to see once again after the last one. Your eyes are as green as your moonlight, a moonlight of your own that you always give me with your hand resting on mine, as if you were gifting me with a future where I am reborn a little more with the beginning of each time with you. A time forever. Like the moon that I keep for you without imprisoning you, without taking away your freedom to leave, but on the condition that it never takes you far away from me.

Your happiness doesn't depend on what you lack, but on what you do with what you have. To tell you the truth, you never lack anything because life always gives you what you need to be yourself. You may not understand its gesture, its intention to help you, because if it always gave you what you wanted, you would end up with very little of what you received. We have been endowed with the purpose of transforming what we need into what we want. It's not an easy task because it asks us to be grateful in the face of pain, scars and suffering, to be able to transform what hurts into what makes us grow, to be able to transform what makes us suffer into a path towards acceptance and consequent change. Everything in life exists so that we can one day live in peace with ourselves. The problem always lies in what we believe about ourselves. If we believe that what happens to us always depends on someone else's will, we will give our lives into the hands of those who never want the best for us. If we are certain that our life is the result of our choices, we realize straight away that nothing happens by chance and that the madness of being ourselves is the healthiest way to avoid being like everyone else.

The best choice is to bring back to life what you've let die inside you. You lost yourself a long time ago because you allowed yourself to ignore your true path. You chose the easiest one, the one you were made to believe was the best without realizing that you were dying a little more while ignoring the days when all the possibilities could still be within your reach, the one you were told would never be the shortest of all the others. You allowed your soul to fall silent, to grow old without wrinkling, to feel tired without making any effort, to cancel itself out in a corner of your silent heart, to let itself be left behind like leaving a fight in the middle for fear of losing what will never be won. To let die what still has life in you is to kill at the same time memory and forgetfulness, desire and urgency, the sun and the moon in your various skies, the waves of the sea that you no longer seek out for fear of not being able to celebrate them, the smiles that you've turned into dead, dry lips just because you're afraid you won't know how to kiss those who have stopped looking for you. You have to start listening to the cry of your life inside you, that cry that burns your veins and tries to thaw your blood, that calls out to you nonstop because it knows that you have so much more to live for, to give of yourself if you don't insist on staying where you are, if you turn your back on others and look for yourself in the places that have been calling out to you for too long. These are choices that only depend on you and no one else. Flights stronger than the wind that drags you without resistance. Absences of what you can still feel without seeing. Things that are yours and nobody else's.

I take you by the shoulders and nestle you in my arms. Your breasts warm my chest and I feel your breath enter me like a question seeking answers. I lift your head with my finger under your chin and smile at you. I draw your desire with a kiss and lean your head on my shoulder. Your tongue plays with my collarbone for a moment, molding it as if it was made of plaster and you say softly that you love me, not as if it was a secret, but as if you didn't want anyone else to know. I don't repeat that I love you, not because I don't love you, but because you know me well enough to know that my silence is also a way of loving you without using words. Without saying another word, we talk with our fingertips. Slowly, I lean you against the wall and with the help of my knee I spread your thighs slightly. I feel you tremble, in what could be mistaken for fear, but which I recognize with generous doses of certainty from other moments like this, perhaps in other places, at other times, but always anticipating what you're going to ask of me next. Without haste, I kiss you for a long time while I feel you draw me into yourself. Becoming one, we eternalize our surrender as if in a pact of life, something that few have access to with our intensity, something that only a few have the chance to experience and feel. Time suddenly ceases to exist and the sound of pieces of skin rubbing against each other, of lips travelling between kisses and bites, of a moist fit shaking in a river of water sounds, of tides and madness, comes to us through our moans. Our bodies ask for an oasis, they clamour for a storm that announces itself without the need for wind or rain, they cry out in pain without pain, they demand strange ways of reinventing themselves and several lives in one, all done on a benign battlefield that ends with no injuries and full of passion. I stare at you in silence as you descend along my body and drink me in with the greed of a snake. Nothing is imperfect with you. Everything condemns me to a miracle before life.

Forgive me for not always trusting you. You're not the problem. The problem is who I sometimes don't think I can be. When life traps me, I'm once again that insecure, fearful child who was rejected and unloved by the person who he wanted to feel loved by the most. In the moments I stop trusting you, I also stop trusting myself, and for a minute everything I've ever experienced with you becomes irrelevant, what you've given me and offered me, what I feel, our butterfly smiles as we learn this new way of flying, our kisses in which our lips turn into tides and perfumes, our words that intersect in a harmony only made of love, moons and stars. When I don't trust you, I die a little more each time and suffer what I shouldn't have suffered, because everything we're experiencing should have become nothing more than the sound of our wings beating as we dance in each other's arms in the night, smiling with our eyes, not depending on anything else, free from what never was and never will be a prison for either of us.

You disappointed me and I didn't know what to say. I trusted you so much that I didn't see the obvious before it happened. Nothing happens out of the blue. There's always a reason behind every attitude, even the thoughtless ones. Nothing is done without thinking, without feeling anything that leads you to do something, a fear, a suspicion, a pain, a memory, something that takes away your judgement for seconds and makes you do what you should never have done. But you did and you broke my heart, you stabbed the most sensitive side of my soul, the one where I had written your name forever, the one where I purposely left the most exposed skin so that you could touch it whenever you wanted with your words of love, the one that had the reddest colour on both sides because it was the one I cared for the most. You disappointed me and I cried, not so much because I lost you, but more because I never expected to lose you. I cried because that's the natural way to begin to heal the soul, to stroke its pain like kissing a sunburnt shoulder, slowly, almost without touching, letting the cold breath moisten the tissues and the filaments, bringing it some relief in the almost imperceptible rush of air that circulates slowly over the burn. You disappointed me and I wanted to be alone, not because alone can seem or be the best, but solely because it's only when I'm alone that I don't let myself go mad from the enormity of the pain. That's me. The same as those who know themselves. The same as someone who knows what they're doing because they've lived through it before.

I'm alone again and I'm afraid. You left on a long announced departure and left me with myself, in my own company, so that the lesson is even more difficult to understand. We always attract what we do to ourselves. We always attract what we need most. We always attract what brings us closer to who we are. Only sometimes, learning hurts a lot, it hurts too much, it hurts in such a way that the pain becomes almost intolerable, unbearable, made up of soundless screams, of butterflies without wings, in pain, in agony, just before they die of sadness because they know they can never fly again. You left never to return, but that doesn't scare me. What really terrifies me is the thought that you left because I couldn't do what was necessary so you'd never think of such an idea, so that loving me would be an unquestionable thing for you, a forever thing, one of those things that we simply know will never happen and that we don't even believe could happen. Like a lack of desire. A deadly disease. An unfinished tattoo on the back of a bare foot.

The hardest thing in life is when your soul asks you to do one thing and your heart asks you to do the opposite. The most complicated thing is when you realize that you will suffer from both choices, but you also know that you have to decide on the right one if you want to stay on your path and no longer allow people to disrespect you. Fear is what often makes you hesitate for too long and prolong the decision to a time when you find it even harder to choose, because you suddenly find yourself enveloped in a sadness that is sadder than sadness itself, a sadness that tastes like sickness, a sadness that at a certain point you no longer know if it belongs to you or if you invented it so you wouldn't go mad. When you love someone and your soul asks you to leave, it's as if they're condemning you to death without killing you, it's as if they're giving you a death that's more painful than death itself, a death filled with love and poison, a death that takes the life inside of you and leaves you breathing on the outside, a death that will accompany you throughout your life like a shadow that you're only allowed to feel and never see. Loving someone who doesn't respect you is like loving a destiny you didn't ask for.

It's realizing that if you want to stay alive, you have to let life take you away from that love, not completely, but only to the point where you discover that you have died without ceasing to live. Loving someone who doesn't respect you is like leaving behind what you thought was eternal, forever and ever, committed to life. A thing of angels and demons. A place where you never wanted to find yourself, but from which you can't leave without at the very least suffering a penance greater than all the pains of your own life combined into one. Not just that, but much more than that. Much more than you ever imagined having to endure.

If it happened to you, it was because it had to happen for you to understand what is best for you. If it happened to you, it was because life knew you needed to feel it and live it. Sometimes it's peaceful and you're hardly aware that it's changing you, but other times it's so painful that you just want to run away from what is already hopelessly chained to your leg. The more you stubbornly want to escape, the more the chain tears your flesh and marks your bones. The more you accept it, the less you feel the grip and the lighter you feel to face the sadness of what you didn't want to be feeling. We can't run away from what finds us. We can only escape what seeks us. And when it's the end that's left, when there's only one thing left, let's treat it as it deserves and we'll come out stronger, better able to smile at ourselves without fear of no longer feeling the smile on our face.

Some days I feel much older than I am. A tiredness comes over me that robs me of my lucidity and throws me on the sofa like a deathly wounded animal. The explanation is easy and I can recognize it in the smallest signs. Only a huge disappointment can for a moment reduce me to a square root elevated to the absurd, to a pain that tears mercilessly through the veins of my soul, to a weariness that couldn't be greater if feigned, to intimate tears that fall like grains of salt on a floor dried by my own panting breath, to a lifeless gaze on my life as if for a moment it didn't even exist. It is always very difficult for me to overcome without some suffering what I thought would never happen, what I believed I would never receive from those who were gone before I even left the place, what I didn't even let into my sleep in nightmares. It's only when I recover what once seemed unthinkable, that silence that always precedes a punch in the heart, a deafness that has finally been cured, two words that make all the difference, a long look beyond the sky, beyond that space where I'm usually reborn, that I finally realize that I needed to live through all this to see myself again, to feel myself, to value myself, to be able to throw myself once more onto the trail of those who live. Nothing else will be able to kill me for long. Nothing will stop me from breathing the air that is mine by right and merit. I remember, with a smile on my lips, my need to face a few misfortunes in order to get closer to who I am, who I should never have stopped being, who I will do everything I can to never be again. Simple but hard thoughts. Like a slap in the dark. A push in the back. A nothing that's worth everything.

Loving someone isn't just loving someone. It's much more than that. Loving someone is waking up without a past and creating a present every day made up of more and more desires, new words and memories, it's trusting as if trusting was as simple as kissing, it's having no urgency for anything because everything is given without being asked, it's offering your skin without fear of seeing it shiver, it's breathing in silence because there's nothing more to say, it's finding in the other person what you didn't even know existed, it's being an angel without fear of flying in the light of an embrace. To love someone is to be everything the other person expects without ceasing to be yourself, it's not having to sacrifice what already belonged to you, it's identifying the flavor of each part of the other person's body as if they had breastfed you with their heart, it's taking a journey through nameless and endless seas and rivers, through stars dazzled by the moon's gaze, it's recognizing the squeeze of fingers on your shoulder and knowing what's next, it's not needing to open your eyes to understand who has them closed. Loving someone is much more than loving someone. It's falling asleep holding hands and waking up without clothes. It's living without secrets. It's not relying on astrologers or fortune tellers and breaking the crystal ball without hesitation. It's having the courage to stop being afraid of losing. It's being a flower in a garden eager for freedom. In a place that's ours and nobody else's. In a place where love has the shape of the soul. Forever. Like in a time that doesn't need time to be time. Like in a time that celebrates us without the need to have us there.

The greatest stupidity is to want to control a relationship or to inflict the same suffering that they inflicted on us. There are many people who say they forgive a betrayal and then don't rest until they feel avenged. There are people who don't deserve to live in a relationship because they only know how to bring insecurity and suffering to the other person. These are people who should be grateful, but who constantly put those they claim to love in a position where they could lose them. And when they lose them, they go crazy with pain, as if they thought life was blind and couldn't give them what they've spent too long taking from others. People who walk without seeing where they're going. People who step on themselves. Like sleepwalkers. Like demons dressed in white.

The worst loneliness is the kind that happens between two people, the kind that robs you of a bit of life every day, the kind that makes you deny what hurts, the kind that blinds you so you don't have to see what you've already seen for a long time. Living with someone who doesn't see you is like being alone holding hands with no one, it's like being deskmates with the fear of being alone, it's not having the courage to tell yourself the truth, that truth that gets further and further away every day, that truth that is so muffled it crushes the heart and gags the soul. To live with someone who doesn't smile at you, who doesn't give you affection, who doesn't have time for you, who criticizes you as if criticism was the same as a dialogue, is to deny who you are, to drown out all the dignity and respect you deserve, to shout cries that you don't even hear because they're so inaudible. Living with someone who makes you feel alone is giving up on living what you came down here to live, it's exchanging freedom for lies, it's having a stump instead of a tongue, it's being poor without being aware of your addiction, it's cowardly disguising life in a lifeless life, in a life in which you've stopped looking so as not to be unlucky enough to find what you know you no longer want to get back.

One day you'll be nothing more than a vague memory, just a space of time during which I believed, mistakenly, as in an illusion, in someone who wasn't prepared to live with me. One day, whole days will pass when I will no longer remember anything that happened between us, as if it all belonged to another life, another story other than my own, a breath of wind that no longer carries your perfume. One day, I won't be able to remember your name, not even if I search the most recondite places of my memory for something that has been lost or that I no longer want to find, as if it was a road that no longer leads anywhere, a place that is no longer of any use, a photo that has lost its sharpness with prolonged exposure to a merciless sun. One day, your face will be just a shadow in the darkness, a confusing series of features that I will no longer be able to put together into one, a question that I no longer want an answer to. One day, it will just be me and no one else, or me and someone else, someone very different from you, someone who will give me what you never knew how to give no matter how much you said you loved me, no matter how much you said everything would be different from now on. One day, I won't even be able to write this again because I won't remember anything, not even what I haven't forgotten yet, what continues to make me suffer in silence. One day, it will just be another day with nothing of you, a day when the sea will no longer remind me of us, a day when I will travel to new places far from the ones I visited with you and where I will smile with another woman with the same joy I did in your company, one day I will be a new me without any more pain caused by you, without any insecurity or disappointment, sadness or fear, which naively or not you provoked in me until the day when my love for me was stronger than the love for who you were with me. One day, you'll be that dream I never dreamt, that book I never took off the shelf, that time with no sign of any life. Just that or not even that. Maybe nothing at all, because then you'll become what you never were, what no longer occupies even my emptiness, not even my greatest sadness, not even the longing I no longer have for what I never experienced with you.

An unhappy person will never make you happy, but rather like themselves. It can't be otherwise. Don't kid yourself that you'll be able to make them happy. Unhappiness is a choice. Those who decide to keep it on their side become addicted to its regrets and silences, its guilt and predictability. It's like a chronic illness, an addiction to life, a poison that no longer kills any more than it already has. Wanting to change it is like wanting to give sight to someone born blind, words to a mute, hearing to someone who can't distinguish the rumble of thunder from a cry of pain. The next thing you know, you've let yourself be infected and you're asking them for the same attention they never gave you, the smile they threw to the bottom of their life, the love that only you believed existed. To stay close to an unhappy person is to want to hide the pity you've always felt for yourself. It's seeing in them what deep down you never stopped being either.

The greatest luxuries you can have are health, love, peace and freedom. The rest are just lies that you keep up in order to be accepted by others, to be admired, to be able to move around in what you believe is your life. Nobody lives without health, love, peace and freedom. Suffering exists in the absence of any of these. Suffering is the result of wanting what is not meant to be with you, of wanting to live what is not for you. Suffering happens because you listen more to others than to yourself, because you'd rather be normal than live the madness of being yourself. Only mad people have the audacity to defy normality and follow the path that no one else chooses, because being mad is not actually being abnormal.

It's just being different from all of those who are content with being the same.

It's very difficult to love someone who loves their freedom, not because it's impossible, but because we have an innate need to control. It's true that we fight this tendency a lot, but in the most difficult or insecure moments we need certainties that escape us through thoughts of indecision and frustration and we end up wanting to know more than what we see. Freedom is very easy to understand, but very complex to accept, precisely because it is what we most desire, but it is also what we most envy. Human beings have characteristics that are difficult to change and one of them is the need to control what they think is theirs and what they love. When what you think is yours and what you love get mixed up with the most primitive emotions that exist deep inside us, we go back to being cavemen, where we ignore the fact that what doesn't add anything to us doesn't subtract anything from us either, where wanting to command is worse than wanting to understand, where in the name of our own happiness we can't take away that of the other. Loving someone free isn't for everyone. It's only for those who fly alongside the other person without wanting to grab them by the wings for an instant until they fall.

When a poet cries, poetry can't help but scream with their pain. They lack a smile and have plenty of tears, but something much deeper crushes their soul. In these moments, the poet silences themselves by writing. They write what few want to read and often what many think they understand. Writing poetry is like flying. It's like hearing voices close to your ear. It's like a mouth that leaves a trail of letters on sheets of paper and builds a ballad just for you, because a poet never writes for others. They always write only for themselves what they let confide in silence with the moon, little secrets revealed with the intensity of the pain of childbirth, confessions spoken with the same beauty of a peaceful gaze that manages to make everything around them disappear. As if by magic. Just with words.

For the first time in my life, I feel deeply in love with a woman. It's a strange thing to say, but it's ultimately the greatest truth

I've ever wanted to be able to write. I feel on the one hand the same as many others, but on the other hand completely different, not only because my love is different from everyone else's, but also because it's mine and she's part of what I've become forever. I've known her for so many years and only now do I understand what I've never seen or what I've always refused to accept, her very own way of smiling at me, hugging me, tolerating me, awakening me to what I only understand today. I let myself travel back in time and revisit every little detail, every touch, every kiss, every look, every word, all with an incredulous and childishly surprised smile, with a completely new lightness that fills my chest as if I was a traveler dressed only in the memory of the warmth of your kisses and lips. My heart gave its name to the wind. It abandoned itself on her skin. I couldn't do it any other way. There was no other way I could show her how she so easily takes me to touch the sky now. How she gives life to what I no longer want to let die in me. How she makes me love so much everything so beautiful that has been created between us.

I realized that you can love someone to the point of total mental imbalance and that didn't scare me. On the contrary. It made me see her as I'd never seen her before, that smile that becomes eternal because it never fades from her face even when she's not smiling, those dreams that were mine alone and that today I can't see myself living without her, the unknown way I look for her even when she's already by my side, the ridiculousness of not being able to find the words to talk about everything I feel, this love that makes me love her down to the last cell, down to the last drop of blood, as if from one day to the next you had become my drug so that I could live, not in dependence, but in incomparable freedom. With her, nothing is ever repeated, even if it seems the same. It's always a new story, a new sea green gaze every time I look at her, angry and calm, with a glow that overwhelms me, that provokes me, that makes me grab her by the shoulders and kiss her without being able to pretend that I love her just a little, that I don't know how to love her too little, that for the first time in my life I don't mind saying that I belong to someone other than myself. I'm suspended in your smile, in your eyes. I become skin of her skin. Beauty of her beauty. And I no longer wish to leave the places where she are not in my thoughts, where the memory of your perfume makes me tremble each time with a desire that overwhelms me with wonder, with a life full of life, hers alone and no one else's.

It's curious that when I finally truly love someone, it's precisely the moment when love risks becoming just a discredited word throughout the world. Men create hatred over lands and flags, threaten each other like betrayed lovers, attack each other without regard for consequences, spit on enemy corpses and hail death like a hymn, turning love into endless suffering, a faithless hope, a strange feeling unfit for dreams, a forbidden feeling almost heralding doom. Now that I love, I can see perfectly well how unreasonable it is to have so much hatred, so much anger built up because you don't have the courage to take the first step in the opposite direction, in the direction of no longer putting off what is most precious in life. Loving someone you once hated is like killing the past without looking back, it's seeing the other person's soul beyond everything else, it's letting the moon be a bridge between two hearts, it's being a poet instead of an illusionist, it's feeling love with every wingbeat. I love because life has given me the grace to meet someone who sets me free without any fear of losing me, someone who holds my hand and tells me I can do it, someone who reminds me of the immortality of everything I feel. Just like the world, which at the moment needs more love and less hate. It needs more sea than fog. It needs someone to remind it that religion and love are not the same thing. That it needs attitudes and not miracles. That it needs to give up understanding what no longer needs to be understood.

What I ask of you most is that you never let go of my hands. I've given you my heart, trembling with fear, because for the first time in my life I love someone. I grew up without a hug, let alone a kiss, and I defended myself for years behind a fearful seduction to never risk rejection. I never chose and I was always chosen. I only liked those who said they liked me first. I didn't risk a millimetre that would bring me closer to possible suffering. I always hid my neediness in an attitude of detachment that gave me a seductive look that confused those who were attracted to me. I didn't win battles or build castles. I just always tried to know the exact amount of time that separated me from the pain in order to avoid it through fantasy dreams and escapes and through labyrinths that I designed on the shifting sands of my life. I know that the future is a horizon that is yet to be seen and that makes me tremble with fear. But I've decided to sail with you, to tear through every wave and face every storm, not to listen to the sirens' tantalizing song and to escape the worst hurricanes, and the thing I ask of you the most is that you never let go of my hands. I may sound ridiculous, but that's not the point. When you love someone, you just want to feel that they give you back what you also feel.

The impossibility of changing something causes a sadness that is hard to explain. When you realize that what you're not allowed to or can't change is because it's supposed to be that way, you're left with a lump of anguish and frustration in your throat. It's only when you can accept that something is here to stay that you can discover the true lesson it brings with it. If, on the other hand, you condemn what is, loneliness immediately takes hold of your heart. The sentence is what prevents you from realizing that loneliness exists only to remind you that if you feel lonely, it's precisely because you've forgotten yourself.

I have a weakness for the unexpected. I love anything that breaks my routine and makes me smile. I'm attracted to difference. I'm a stickler for the truth and I hate gossip and judgement. I like to approach everything with an open mind and have no patience for people who constantly victimize themselves. I don't put much stock in plans, because I like to follow ideas, impulses and adventures. I love to laugh and have a good drink with friends. I hate breadcrumbs and lack of respect. I'm not looking for relationships, but connections. I run away from normality because it kills the madness of my naturalness. I'm not afraid of breaking my heart. I'm more afraid of not feeling it break.

Open up to the sky. Accept what you're experiencing so that you can live in peace and transform everything into energy of acceptance. Accept your reality so that your heart can open up to something else that can only inevitably come from you. If you accept what you're experiencing, you can finally change your attitude. If you accept what you're experiencing, you can finally grow. If you accept what you're experiencing, you'll enter the dimension of your soul and nothing will ever be the same in your life.

What I want most in a woman is for her to give me peace. My wish may sound strange, but I know what I'm talking about. I can only find peace in a woman who is at peace with herself, at peace with her life, at peace with our love. Only that and so much at the same time. Mutually. Always for both sides.

Everything we feel we need exists within us. In fact, a desire is nothing more than a preference for something that we already have, even if we don't know it. A desire is never a need, nor is it a choice. A desire is a request from the soul to turn inwards. In fact, a wish is the beginning of all our creations. The great question that life asks of us is precisely to know what our greatest desires are and to make them our reality. Only then will we be able to experience the joy of also being an intimate part of those same desires.

Nothing that you intimately feel you are has ever ceased to be. You may still be unaware of it, but the truth is that it has always existed within you. When you decide to dive inside, everything is revealed to you through what you feel. Don't be afraid to go inside your chest and listen. Don't be afraid of not hearing anything, because that's where your heart and your inner voice are. You'll always hear what you need to hear, you just can't give up at the first attempt. You're not used to concentrating on yourself. Insist and you'll end up with the answers you always knew you were looking for. You'll recognize them from all the others you've been given. You'll feel them as your own. Then all you have to do is follow them, without fear of failure or being wrong, and life will be yours forever.

Don't wait for what's not for you. Face everything that comes your way and learn from it. Don't repeat the same choice so you don't fall into the same situation. Be free and don't judge, because when you judge you deny the evidence and believe you know everything that others don't know. The truth is that you don't know any more than you need to know in order to enter the new stage that will take you a little further along your path.

Stop torturing yourself with what others do to you. Realize that they're just people bringing you a message. Realize that they're just people who have come to teach you to respect yourself even more and to not worry so much about other people's opinions.

All your greatest truths lie within you. Don't look for them outside, because you'll only be moving further away from your path. Your greatest guidelines are given to you only by your soul and your intuition. Never underestimate them, because it's time to start valuing who you are.

My life is sustained by not knowing what lies ahead, by not knowing what will happen next. It may sound crazy, but predictability has always left me with a sick feeling in my stomach. I much prefer not knowing anything so that I can experience everything with the blessing of surprise. I know that many people don't understand me, but I don't want to teach anyone anything either. What makes me happy is that I no longer have to fight for anything, because I realize that this way only what is for me stays with me. The rest, what I sometimes want without needing, no longer makes me throw my life up in the air just to see which way it turns this time.

People don't want to hurt you. They simply don't like what you awaken and make them feel inside with your behaviour. From here, they throw their pain and frustration at you and accuse you of what you cause them. You just have to understand this and protect yourself. The rest will depend solely on how disrespectful you allow them to be towards you.

Only your love for you can save you from yourself. Learn to believe in what you feel deep down inside. Stop doubting who you can become. Imagine your greatest dream and smile. Seize the opportunity that life has given you to be here, now, and make your way. If you don't make this decision, you'll never find the best of you.

Think about what you have difficulty facing and think about doing it. You'll feel fear, but that's okay. Let it grow in your chest, let it take hold of you. Then feel the pain of that fear and cry if you feel like it. Crying helps to release the pain and draw strength from it. Tomorrow, do the same and you'll realize that it hurts less. The day after tomorrow, do it again and you won't be so afraid of that pain. The truth is that if you don't stop doing it every day, one day you'll end up feeling peace, purely and simply because you've finally understood why it exists and you're no longer afraid of it.

Be born again to a new life. Don't let yourself die without living. Live without fearing death. Remember that many die while still alive and others die without having lived. Commit to yourself in life so that you live without dying, even if you know that one day you'll have to leave. Dare to pursue what makes you feel alive and have the courage to trust in life. Believe that nothing will ever match what you believe to be your biggest and wildest dreams.

Obstacles aren't meant to make you give up. They exist to not make you give up. Life will test you until you know that you will no longer give up on your commitment to not forgetting yourself. Don't fear or give in to your biggest obstacles, as long as you realize that they come to help you and not to set you back. Don't wish to dominate them. Accept them as ways to realize your strength and determination. That's why you find them. That's why you attracted them.

Only a soul can sense where someone else's soul is. Only a soul can make another soul shine. Where there is no soul, there is logic. Sometimes you think you're touching someone with your soul when in fact you're wanting them to do what you believe is best for them. A soul doesn't convince any other soul. A soul makes another soul choose for its own energy, choose only what has to do with itself.

Life is a blessing. Break the rules. Dare to love without fear. Have fun without measure. Take responsibility without fearing it. Take risks. Laugh a lot. Follow your impulses. Dream big. Do what you're passionate about. Change for your own sake. Live where you like. Stay only where you feel like staying. And never listen to those who tell you otherwise, because they're always the ones who wish you were like them.

Take responsibility for your life today, now, and change direction. No more postponements and excuses. Face the disapproval of others. Face yourself. Forget about fear and face what lies beyond that gaze of yours resting on the ground. Raise it, at the same time calmly and promptly. Look at what's in front of you and take the first step. Life is waiting for you. Don't make it wait any longer. Grant yourself the right to start living again today.

I have things in my heart that nobody taught me about life. I learned them for myself. They are very much my own forms and ideas, intrinsic to my way of thinking and being. I stopped listening to others a long time ago in order to listen more to myself. I decided to start living again, this time without reins or restrictions. I became free by choice. I finally claimed my space. I started to believe only in what transforms me and I stopped looking at what I aspire to, because what I aspire to is not always what transforms me. Quite the opposite. Usually, what I aspire to is almost always what destroys me.

Life doesn't let you see what you're not supposed to find yet. Don't be afraid of not knowing, but rather of not being open to understanding. When you make a choice, commit to it so that you can take responsibility for its consequences. No matter what anyone tells you, believe only in what you originate, because only that reflects your truth. If you want to change your truth, change your attitude and stop trying to prove to others what you don't believe yourself to be. Happiness also starts that way.

I always find it very difficult to contradict myself. I believe in what I choose as much as in what I let go. I don't waste a lot of time trying to understand what's not being revealed. I am a companion to all those who respect me and know how to listen. My rebellion is more that of someone who sees themselves in what they feel. I don't fear rejection and I understand it now more than I ever have in my life. I'm friends with my friends as long as they ask before passing judgement. I need my truth to uncover other people's lies about me. I have desires that I won't give up, precisely because I find in them the reason for wanting them so much. I love venturing out to where the adventure ends and the dream begins, and I've stopped looking in others for what I need most for myself.

I love people in love. I love people who, against everything and everyone, live great loves. I love people who share secret loves. I love people for whom age and social status are no impediment to great passion. I love people who hug and kiss. I love people who travel together without a destination. I love people who like the same music and books. I love people who like people. And above all, I love people who fall in love with the same person every day.

Most of the answers lie in what you hide in the questions you ask. If you're not honest, you get dishonesty. If you want to please in order to be accepted, you end up being left behind. If you're afraid of not being loved, you always end up being betrayed. If you fear being judged, you end up being humiliated. Realize that the important thing is to understand the emotion behind each choice. Don't choose anything out of fear, because you'll always lose something you love. Choose out of love. Choose what makes you smile so that you can reverse the answers and change the questions. That way, you'll definitely be hearing what you need to hear.

I like feelings that have reasons that start in the eyes. I like gestures that first touch the smile. I like things that are as unlikely as they are absurd and that disturb me without really disturbing me. I like to forgive without knowing if I'll remember the forgiveness. I like people like me who like people like them. I like people who love people who don't deserve it, just because they need it. I like people who don't ask questions because they don't live with answers. I like those who don't fear the possibility of new love and toast all those they've lived with. I like to like without necessarily being liked.

It's time to read your thoughts. It's time to understand what you really want and don't want in your life. You're unhappy and lost. Your time seems to fly by and you're unable to manage it so that you have more time for yourself. You live with expectations about almost everything and only get disappointments and a feeling that you're passing life by. It's time to get emotional with yourself and realize where you need to start making different choices. It's time to say "no" to others so that you can say "yes" to yourself much more often.

The secret of genius is to see what nobody else sees. The spirit of genius is to not mind looking ridiculous or crazy. The truth is that all genius always has a large dose of ridiculousness and madness, precisely because it takes us where few others even try to go. To be a genius is to have the ability to understand error and failure, as well as sameness and predictability, and not want to stay with either of them. To be a genius is above all to be aware of the ability to create what no one else dares or imagines they can change.

Stay still. Rest. Don't do anything. Today is the time to give yourself time. Don't demand anything that causes you effort. Today is the time to let everything go without lifting a finger. Today is the time to realize who and what wants to stay with you and by your side. Don't be afraid of losing anything or anyone, because in reality you only keep what you're meant to keep. Let go of what you're afraid to let go of. Release everything that holds you back. Today is the time to stop and feel. Today is the time to change your choices and take new paths.

You can be sure that what makes me who I am is not so much the courage to be myself, but rather the passion to want to be myself more and more, above all knowing how to live with my feet on the ground and my soul always touching the sky, where I came from and where I will surely return to one day.

I love inventing crazy things that aren't about love. What's marvellous doesn't necessarily have to be loved. I remember things that somehow became unforgettable in my life without being for love. I remember divine drinks on nights when I was a DJ without knowing how I managed to be one. I remember moonlit nights in the dunes on the beach, lying on my back, talking to myself and counting the stars so I wouldn't fall asleep. I can no longer forget my teenage outbursts of fear written in the form of poems that I read solemnly to my totally stoned friends. I remember the big fashion falls from which I emerged miraculously unscathed and laughing in a stupid mixture of relief and foolishness. To tell the truth, I found in each of these follies the adventure of not wanting to find answers, but just having fun. Love, however, was postponed in time, not out of fear, but because at the time pain still had no place in my heart.

At a time when hardly anyone cares to understand why you're here, I'm making a difference. I want to activate my sensitivity more and more in order to understand and get a sense of myself. If I feel afraid, I move forward. If they want to stop me, I draw my sword and don't back down. Nothing stays the same in my life when I don't give up on myself. Everything gets my smile. Everything gets my touch. Everything becomes part of me. Everything makes me believe that to understand myself is to push my limits and fall in love with my talents. Amen.

I have an immature side that only manifests itself in my maturity. I don't know how to just be more or less of someone. I need my immaturity to be more than what I need to be. I want to be who I haven't yet been in order to get where I never thought I'd go. Being immature gives me the courage I need to dare to face all the fear that makes me an orphan in life. I love setting aside prudence and reasonableness and living in a way that only I know. It's my rebellious side and averse to tombs of irony and lies. I want to burst into laughter and redesign all my dreams. It's time to be immature once again. Tonight, I set off on a new, long journey to happiness. This time, with no turning back.

I've lived arm in arm with the pain of living without understanding why everything had to happen the way it did. Not knowing my truth made me believe lies for far too long. Suffering competed with me for a front seat. Fortunately, I collapsed and became depressed. I fell so I could rest. I let myself stay on the ground so that I could breathe again without pain. I got up slowly, a little each day, until I was able to sit down and look out of one of the windows of my house. It was a time of heroics and giant steps over the weakness of not being able to do much. One day, I smiled again and realized that it had all been worth it. I realized that every pain has a story and every story has a reason for its pain. Mine had to do with respect. With a lack of respect for me.

I'm good because I'm good to myself. I'm no more or less than anyone else. I'm incomparable, and anyone who doesn't understand what I mean by these words doesn't realize what they're doing here. Anyone who compares themselves to me misses out on the best of themselves. Tell me to fuck off if you want, but don't say "fuck off" to what I make you feel. What you feel when you look at me, the anger, the injustice, the insecurity, the frustration, the love, the fear, is nothing of what I have to give you, but of what you need to work on in yourself. Shit on me, because I'm nobody compared to you. You're special to yourself and you don't need anything more than what I'm making you feel. If it hurts, go inside. If it makes you afraid, face it and understand. If it makes you angry, stop and feel what your chest is telling you. I'm nobody to you, but I can make you look inwards simply by existing. You will do the same to others. And even others to other ones. That's how life works. You don't always get what you want, but you always get what you need. Cheers.

Most people insist on teaching you what doesn't work for them. It may sound stupid, but it's their way of feeling capable of doing something that gives them some meaning in life. In reality, they do what they do because they don't believe in themselves and want others to see them as they never were. Teaching what you don't do is the same as saying what you don't believe in. It works as a way of praising what doesn't exist, of showing what was never there, of kneeling down just for fear of being chastised. Nobody can be what they're not for long. Everything falls apart without warning and you find yourself exposed to the ridicule of being found out without actually having committed any crime or theft. They just wanted to be someone to those around them, someone to those they think love them, all in a sad and mediocre life choice that leads nowhere. Life asks us to be true, simple, loyal to our soul, but the vast majority run away from the little that is asked of them and prefer to invent lies that give them the illusion of gaining time and conquering dreams. The vast majority seem to forget that the worst lie is always the one they tell themselves, because it gives them an excuse not to live their truth.

If you came to visit me today, I promise I could smile at you. Maybe I'd even offer you a glass of champagne to celebrate our reunion. I haven't seen you for too long. My heart is tired of beating without feeling you by its side. I daydream and imagine you everywhere in the house you used to live in. I've been out very little since you left. I'm afraid you'll decide to turn up and I won't be here at that time. If you came to visit me today, I know you'd tell me why you left, because I also know you don't want to go on thinking what you think. I know you don't want to hurt me, but I also know you don't want me enough to come back. However, I know that if you came to visit me today, it would be the same as telling me you were ready to come back. Without fear. Perhaps without much love. But surely with the memory that you haven't forgotten the taste of salt on the skin of your lips when we kissed for the last time.

All losses are a guide that life gives you to correct your choices and directions. Losing a mum or dad may not be about changing your life. It may just be so that you can learn to live without them in the pain of no longer being able to count on their company, a way of turning inwards to find yourself in the sadness you've never felt before. New emotions lead to discoveries about yourself that you would otherwise never be able to feel. It's a kind of storm without wind, a downpour without water, a prayer that opens your heart to what you couldn't see before and are now beginning to understand. In fact, losing is a chance to gain a new path, a new direction, a new voice, a new freedom. It's taking a loving punch from life to make you realize how far you are from who you should be, who you should be with and where you should be. It's shaking you up inside so that you can finally feel and hear your wings beating outside. It makes you admire what no longer transcends you. Just that and so much at the same time.

I dance alone to forget you, I dance because with every step I move away from who I was with you, who I let myself be because I wanted you so much, because I let my heart ache so much. I dance in silence so that the sound of my breathing prevents me from repeating your name over and over again, I dance until I can no longer feel the rhythm or the beat of the notes that I no longer hear anywhere but in the rumor of my thoughts trying to escape from you, from your memory, from your laughter, the way you lied to me saying you loved me like you'd never loved anyone else, the way you hid the truth from me with kisses on the ear and bites on the lips, the firm way you lowered my eyelids with your fingertips wet with my tears and told me everything was fine, when everything had been wrong for a long time. I didn't want to see it, I didn't want to accept it, not even when you didn't look for me like you used to, not even when you disappeared without telling me where you were hiding, who you were meeting in secret, in the darkness of the long nights without you and the dawns made cold by your absence. I dance alone without stopping to forget that you ever existed by my side, so that I can convince myself that I only dreamt a nightmare and that I have now woken up in a new time where I alone belong to this existence. To this haunting. To this fuzzy memory that loses its lustre with every scream I hold back in my swollen throat from silencing what I so desperately want to say, as if the words were open wounds by the ones I no longer hear, the words I want to forget like someone who wakes up without waking up, like someone who dies without dying. I dance and I will dance until this dance makes me fall over with exhaustion, makes me lose my sight and my ability to remember memories, throws me into a corner of another corner and makes me forget that I ever loved those who contaminated me with love, those who made me part of the past without ever making me part of the present, those who presented me with pain as if it was a life forever.

There is so much falsehood among people that walking alone doesn't seem so hard. There is so much talk of understanding, love and gratitude, but more and more selfishness is encouraged as a way of getting what you want more easily. Dishonesty is practised like a religion, a secret and personal cult that is waved like a victorious flag. Lies have become so widespread among people as if they were truths that you want to believe them, to let them run a life of illusion where the end is inevitably a fall without being able to put your hands in front of your face. Nothing seems to make sense other than success, gain, conquest. Nothing seems worthwhile if it doesn't bring with it the certainty of turning hours into minutes, silences into words, darkness into light, fears into laughter, disappointments into victories, as if life was a game where only the clever and not the daring win. Being honest is becoming a rarity, almost a loser's label, when in fact we forget that telling the truth about what we feel and think is the only way to get to where we're not curious about the destination, because regardless of what it is, it will surely be the one we've always hoped to live, the one where the closeness of the unknown paradoxically makes us smile with confidence, the one where we don't need to look like who we're not and where we feel brave enough to go ahead without fear of dying alone. Things of faith, time and love. For ourselves. Unique and forever.

Don't believe the words of someone who has never been in love, because they lack truth and life, they lack everything that only love can give you, they lack the intensity and daring of someone who knows what it's like to want someone very much, the courage to not be afraid of emotions and feelings that can make you suffer, the ability to know that what is thought before being said is always a sum of what can be attributed to others and what we will never be able to explain. Those who have never been in love haven't yet realized that they have never been alive, that what they say doesn't correspond at all to what they would like their reality to be, that not only films and books can create a generous and worthwhile existence. Someone who has never been in love is like someone who has never brought anything to life, someone who only complies and doesn't dare break rules and dogmas, someone for whom the stars are nothing more than bright spots in a sky they don't feel is theirs, someone who doesn't recognize themselves except in what doesn't belong to them. Don't believe the words of someone who has never been in love, because they are words without soul or heart, words spoken only to fill an emptiness that grows in proportion to the time they continue to allow themselves to die in life. Words without passion, without vigor. Words battered with sadness and less noisy than their own silence. Worthless words, invented as if in mute homage to what you don't know and will never know if you don't have the audacity to beat your chest until your heart beats bravely again, without fear of stopping, in a secret desire to live everything you've never been able to be before.

Sometimes you don't need a new path, but to relearn how to walk, to start making choices based on your truth, only your truth, and to live the consequences of these new choices without fear or expectations. A whole different life awaits you, a whole experience never lived before awaits you like a love found at last, a love for yourself that has no measure, no time or space, it happens naturally as if it had always been there, as if you recognized it long before you were living it, like a state of madness, a kind of dementia that no longer has the strength to suffocate your will. To relearn how to walk is to be reborn in another place, to stop living in the company of shadows and welcome a light that doesn't blind you, to risk being defeated but where even defeat is a victory for you, to forgive yourself without having to suffer, to fail and always try again, to know that no one will be able to keep you from what has always been yours. No matter how hard you try. No matter how much you want to.

It hurts so much to suffer for love. It's probably the pain that hurts the most, the pain that burns the most, the pain that tears the most, the pain that shatters the most intimate part of us, that place that few access and even fewer remain in. The truth is that it hurts so much to suffer for love. It's like a match that burns endlessly inside your chest, a pain that makes you fold in on yourself, a shard of suffering driven deep into your heart, a dark angel that squeezes your veins with the cruelty of a faceless demon. It hurts so much to suffer for love. It's like a disease that currently has no cure or remedy, a land that shouldn't be on any map, a sadness that is sadder than any other sadness, a sadness that makes itself present without being invited, an intruder that we can't kick out of the house, a torture carried out with the same constant and merciless rhythm that always accompanies a loss, a disappointment or a betrayal. It hurts so much to suffer for love because it's supposed to hurt so much so that we remember ourselves once again, who we really are, what we allowed and shouldn't have allowed, what we gave up without thinking about anything, what we denied in ourselves and forgot in the other, what we consented to between the desires and promises we made ourselves and never kept, what should never have existed and what existed only to kill us. If it hurts so much to suffer for love, it's because we deserved it, it's because we should have understood it, it's because we should have chosen to fall asleep alone with the edge of the blanket between our thumb and index finger. Just that and everything would have been different. Everything would have been what it should have been. And nothing else.

Eyes never need subtitles, they speak without using words, without needing silences or shouts, kisses or lights, darkness or winds. Eyes speak in the way they look, that's all. They speak with the intensity of their glare, with the almost imperceptible movements of the iris and eyelids, with the twinkle of their smile. Nothing more than that. They always speak without ever ceasing to see. Without ever stopping looking. Without anything changing or anything ceasing to happen.

I abhor normality, because only those who are afraid of living are normal, of daring to go where few go, of flying even if they don't know if they have wings, of the judgement and approval of others, of dancing in the rain, of kissing a stranger for the pleasure of breaking rules and prohibitions, of drinking until you stop feeling the kiss and the hand that caresses you between the thighs, of speaking what you feel and not running away from the consequences, of travelling without a destination and without a place to stay, of writing what no one will want to read, of defending a cause against all those you love, ignoring pain to help someone else suffer less, not having to complain to get attention, wanting to be desired and not hiding your desire, loving without being loved, following what your soul asks of you without hesitation, smiling until your lips hurt, to sleep on the cold sand of a beach on a summer's night, to swim without clothes in a rough sea, to be free even where you're not allowed to talk about freedom, to cry in front of people who don't love you, to get a tattoo all over your face, to live in a house without doors, to laugh at yourself. Normality is for those who don't have a broad mind. It's for those who, if they could, would attend their own funeral.

When you want to please everyone, you're very little of everything and a little of almost nothing. Your individuality simply doesn't exist because your choices are made solely to win everyone's approval and avoid anyone's rejection. The idea that someone might not like you is like an open wound on your breath, something that tortures you like a plague, a curse that has been placed on you for life. You need to be liked simply because you don't love yourself, nor do you know how to do it or deserve it. On the contrary. You subject yourself to incredible situations in the name of an acceptance that you think you have, but which in the end is nothing more than an interest that others may have in you for a while. When you feel they're slipping away, you do everything you can to get back what you never had, what never belonged to you, what only fuelled the illusion that you were loved, desired and wanted. Wanting to please everyone is like a death sentence, a pit full of ghosts, a habit of insignificance, a failure of repetition, a waiting for what isn't waiting for you, a strange way of wanting to remain in a hell with no flames and no end. A hell invisible to the eye. Invisible to the soul. A path at the bottom of the depths.

It's not you who changes life, but life that changes because you have changed. Whatever you do, it will always be the result of your choices. Life is yours and it only becomes different when you make different decisions. Don't delude yourself with truths that aren't yours. They don't change your life, they just create a reality that seems to belong to you, but in reality only leads to more lies and illusions that delay what should already be happening to you. When you change consciously, when you choose with your soul, when you follow what has to do with you, life becomes a reflection of you, a mirror of your gaze, an alchemy without mistakes, a story with meaning, a deep dive into your essence, and everything finally seems to have a meaning, a reason for being, an unforgettable taste, an avenue of life just for you. Change only for yourself and never for others, even if they call you selfish or tell you that you're insensitive. Never forget that you can only give who you are. You can only give your own brilliance and nothing more.

A lie produces unthinkable consequences in the life of the person who tells it, more than in the life of the person who hears it. The liar has no idea of the implications of a lie, of the changes it brings to his existence, of the painful paths that will cross his path from then on, paths he can't escape if he wants to keep lying and not fall into denial of his own words. Lying is manipulating what you don't want to be true, it's not believing in life after death and the consequences that drag on from life to life until you accept the truth without fear of the pain it will bring. Almost every lie brings a new lie, just as our childhood stays with us until we die, whether it was pleasant or terrible, made up of lies or truth, purposely regretted or forgotten, shouted or altered. Lying is a consequence of the childhood we had, a desire to want what we never had and wanted so much, a yesterday that was never today, a reality created to hide what we really think about ourselves. To lie is to fear that the truth will make us suffer. It's drinking without ever getting drunk enough to remember when it all started. It's enduring in silence the pain of truths never spoken. It's keeping with you a haunting masquerading as virtue. Or even worse.

You're right to dislike me. I didn't change to please you. You did everything you could to make me who you wanted me to be, to give you what you thought you were entitled to, to obey you as if obeying you wasn't an obligation, but a choice. You wanted me to speak what you wanted to hear, to smile the smiles you thought you deserved, to always guess what you were missing, to avoid what you wanted to forget. You wanted me to annul myself through your will, to endlessly repeat what you liked to hear, to stop being myself to be who I didn't want to be, to deify you more than your own God. You wanted everything without being able to lose anything. You even wanted what could never exist. You wanted and forgot what I didn't want. You wanted it, but you didn't remember that it's not you who changes people, but people who change according to what you do. You wanted it so badly that you lost. You overdid it so much that I couldn't stand it any longer and left. Never to return. To recover from you. To take in what even you can't take away from me. To fly again in the freedom of those who can't imagine being without it.

It's not true that love cures everything. Love can't cure a lie. It doesn't cure dishonesty. It doesn't cure disrespect. It doesn't cure betrayal. Love only heals what still has love in it. That's it. Nothing else.

Never confuse waiting with wasting time. When you wait, you continue to live everything else that is part of your life without the wait becoming an obsession, a drama more typical of those for whom their existence has no meaning or purpose. When you wait, you don't waste time. On the contrary. You find time that you didn't even know you had in order to gain more time, you anticipate any expectations, you travel without having to leave the place where you create dreams and desires, all those things that inevitably end up being part of who you are. To wait consciously is to not be afraid of what may come, to live peacefully even if alone, to feel a freedom as strong as that of conquests, to smile at everything that has brought you this far. On the other hand, when you waste time, it's because you're where you're not supposed to be, it's because you've reduced yourself to who you shouldn't be, it's because you've become a lover of hate and anger, it's because you've turned all your failures into a single desire for solitude. Nothing in life is achieved without waiting for its own time to happen. It may take more or less time to happen, but you can be sure that it will arrive without transcending or disappointing your will. It will arrive when you let time take care of your time.

The more you simplify life, the less complicated loving yourself will seem. Nobody can love themselves without simplicity, without haste, in lightness of spirit. It's almost like a mathematical equation, a triangle of fire from which no one can escape, a certainty of being certain, a greater evidence than the existence of something we can't see, but which transcends us. To love yourself is to respect your own rhythm, to listen attentively to your soul, to ignore the noisy cries of your brain, to know how to say "no" to your heart even if you may suffer, to not allow anyone to tell you who you are not. To love yourself is to refuse normality and mediocrity, the more or less, and the intolerable, control and hell in life. It's choosing to plant a flower instead of plucking it from the very earth that desperately embraces it to keep breathing life into it. It's as simple as that. Like everything that heals itself.

To witness the birth of a dragon from within a woman is to watch her painstakingly give birth to a new life, to feel her realize for the first time in her arms the touch of her sensitive and intuitive side, her female side, her side capable of doing anything she dreams of and wants, her side bold enough to cuddle the newborn and still untamed animal against herself and fearlessly feel its breath begin to be hers for ever and ever. Nothing is the same in your life from that moment on. Everything takes on a different rhythm, a flavor of desire and unwritten words, everything becomes a journey that begins unhurriedly and yet full of inspiration and lightness, a journey that takes you where you never thought you could go, a journey that makes you realize that you no longer need to keep the lights off to let yourself grow old more quickly, a journey that gives you the courage to no longer want to be upset by what doesn't do you any good or add anything to you. There is a time for everything, but to see the birth of a dragon from inside a woman is to witness a unique moment, hers alone and no one else's, as if she was inheriting a new skin, a new smile, a new body, a new path so different from all those she had traveled up to that moment, a path that is still a happy ending to an impossible love, a love for herself that is born and spreads like a breath of life to be lived, a breath of life where she no longer needs to hide from the world what should never have remained hidden inside her for so long.

Secrets make you sick. Keeping a secret is like feeling alone in a crowd, it's knowing that you're carrying a truth that can change lives. It's like a silent pain that deafens your ears, a scream that you can never shout, loud tears that no one can hear, days lost between what you must do and what you want to do. The worst secrets are the ones you have with those you share your life with. They're worse than secrets. They are sentences that prevent us from living who we are with whom we are with, that make us smile without reason or desire, moments when we feel like saying everything and starting everything without having anything else, any more secrets, any more pain, anything else that hurts us and suffocates the words we don't dare say for fear of their consequences. To have secrets is to have illnesses without a cure, to have no peace of mind about ourselves, to suffer without any wounds on our skin. To have secrets is to burn your soul with ice. It's writing a story made up of nothing but lies.

Don't waste your life living with those who want you to be like everyone else. You'll never be who you want to be because someone doesn't want to see you shine because you overshadow their own frustration at not being like you. Some people exist only to put others off, to make them insecure, to cancel out their essence, their free way of living and flying. They are people who can only give you who they are and nothing more, people who are more concerned with destroying than building, with drowning than teaching you how to swim, with lying than offering the truth, with limiting you so that you don't darken the one who claims to love you. They are people you must escape, to whom you owe nothing but compassion, whom you must leave behind to follow your own path among the stars, among new places and adventures, without shadows or mistrust, just you and your soul together to begin what has not yet begun, together to leave the places cursed by the presence of those you don't want by your side for another day, another second. Together to understand what they didn't let you understand before.

There's nothing more painful than missing what you no longer want to experience. It's a conflict between what you don't want to remember and what you never want to forget. It's like crying without tears, shouting without being able to break any silence, wanting something to end when in fact it shouldn't have ended at all. It's like a pain without a wound, a name you can't speak no matter how much you hear it inside your head, a scar hidden by your fingertips so that no one can see it reopen and bleed. To miss what you no longer want to live is to become a widow without any dead people, to not want or be able to stop yourself from slowly tearing your chest open with each memory that you don't repress because you want it to happen again, even though deep down you know that it won't happen again. There's nothing more painful than missing what you no longer want to experience, not because it can't happen again, but because repeating what makes you suffer is the same as seeming little while being so much, in what was big and you want to seem small, in what has defined you for so long and can no longer mark you. It's being forbidden to love those you still love. It's not being able to be who you always wanted to be. It's having to forget what is still very much alive in your heart, where butterflies kill each other like impossible dreams. All this and much more. Beyond the bearable. Beyond the sustainable.

Some people question my work because of what I write. Others say I live in an unrealistic and crazy world. Others say I'm arrogant and narcissistic. There was a time when all this made me sad. Today, I don't care what anyone thinks about me. I've learned to decide and choose what I want in my life. I've become an even more conscientious and daring person. I challenge those who come to me to go where they've never gone before and to face their greatest fears. I like to constantly provoke people, because I believe in provocation as a way of bringing out the best in ourselves. And above all, I am a successful man, not in relation to others, but in relation to myself and everything I give myself to in the name of a passion that is impossible to define.